Orig

First Published 2022
© text Ioan Morris, 2022
© illustrations Josh Hicks, 2022

No part of this publication may be reproduced, stored in a retrieval system, or transmitted, in any form, or by any means, electrical, mechanical, photocopying, recording or otherwise without the prior permission of the publisher or a licence permitting restricted copying.

ISBN 978-1-914303-20-3

Published by Llyfrau Broga Books, Whitchurch, Cardiff

www.broga.cymru

Orig

The Fearless Life of Orig Williams

Written by Ioan Morris
Illustrated by Josh Hicks

Orig was a born fighter. He grew up in the 1930s in Ysbyty Ifan, a small village in the mountains of Snowdonia that had once been a hideout for robbers.

It was a place where quarrels were common and strongmen were heroes. Someday Orig would become a hero too.

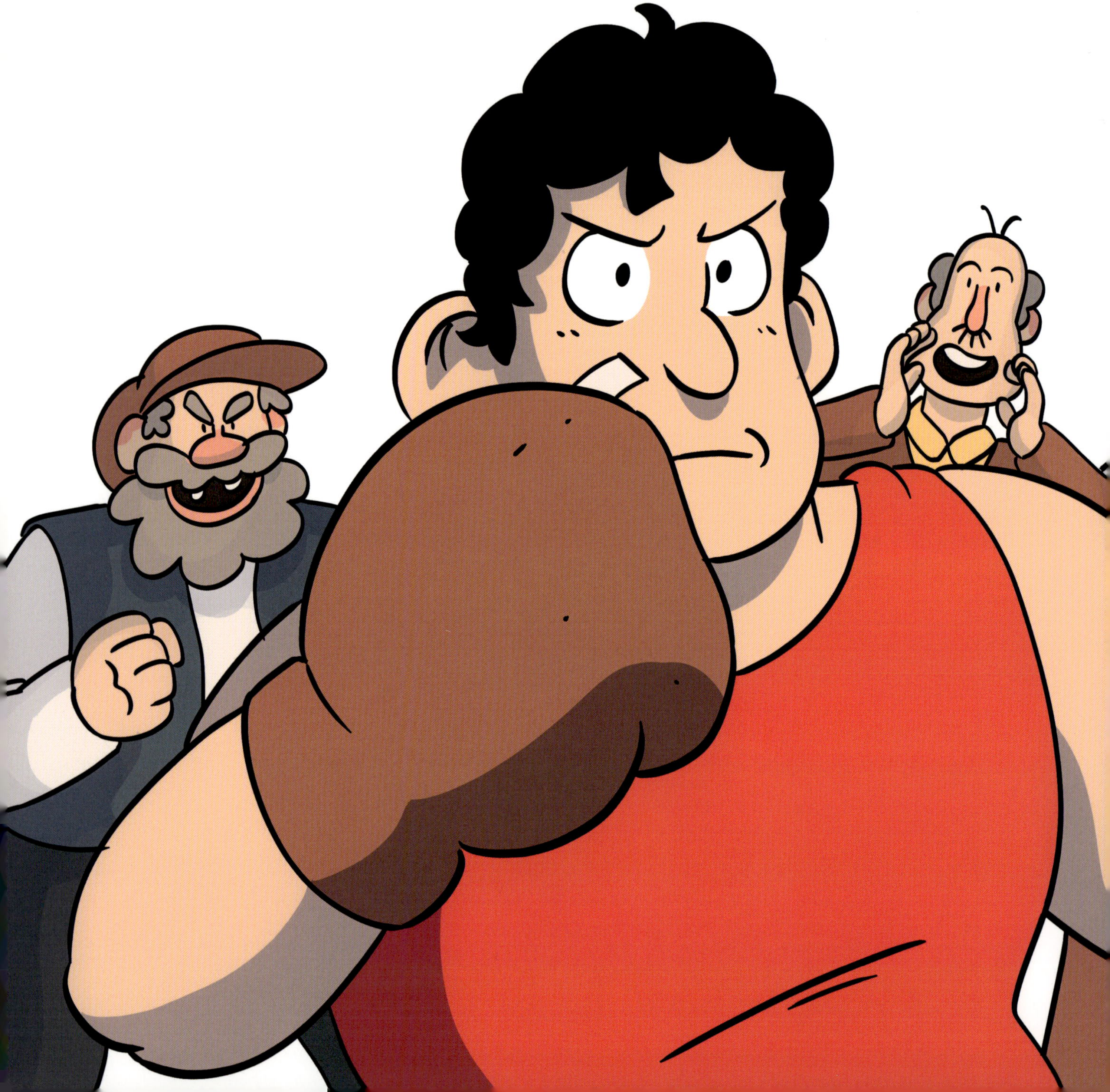

As a boy, Orig enjoyed reading stories and poems, but more than anything he liked sport.

He was a talented footballer and when he was a little older he started boxing.

He was brave even then.

Orig joined the Royal Air Force after leaving school. He didn't enjoy it, but he was able to keep fit and play as much sport as he wanted.

He worked hard to improve and became good enough at football to sign for a professional club.

Orig played for several clubs, including Oldham Athletic and Shrewsbury Town in England and Bangor City and Nantlle Vale in Wales.

He was happy to break the rules to help his team win and he often fought on the field. This led to many red cards and injuries, which put an early end to his playing career.

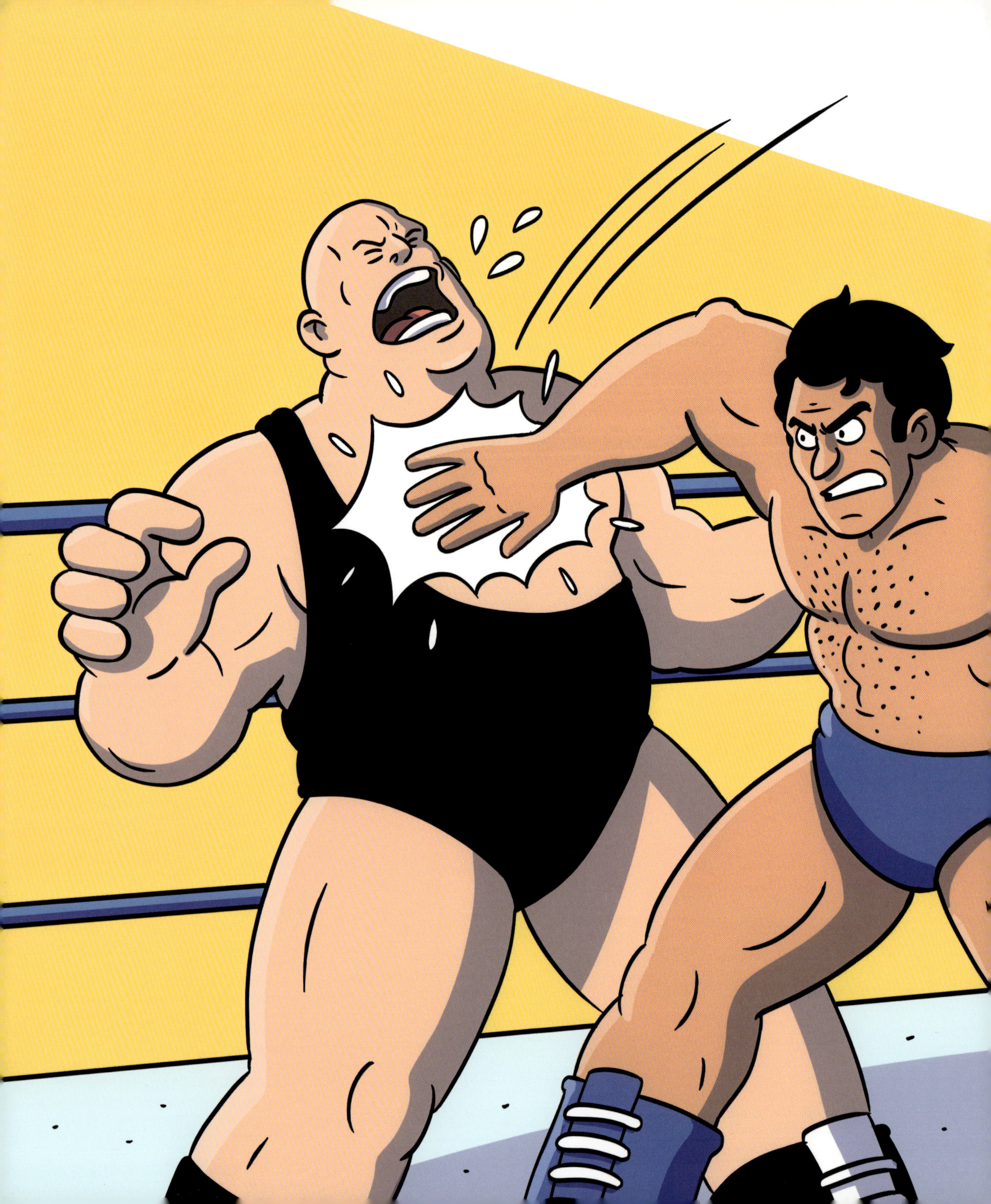

After football, Orig wanted to try something different.

Wrestling had become very popular and Orig realised that if he was a wrestler he would be able to make a living from fighting.

From that moment his life took a new direction.

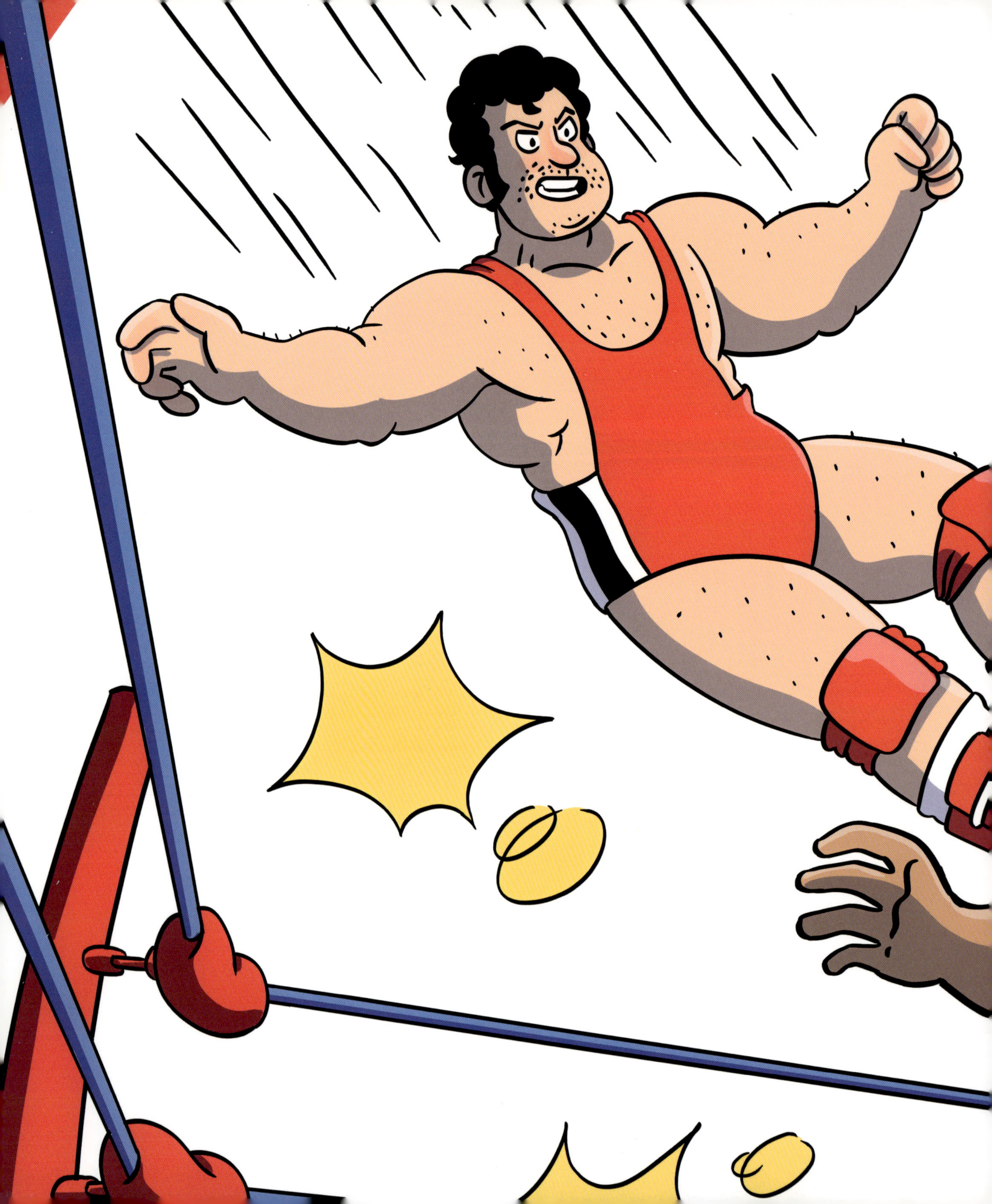

Orig learned how to suplex, slam and dropkick, and he was soon performing in halls and fairgrounds all over Britain and Ireland.

It didn't matter if Orig was wrestling one-on-one, or with a partner in a tag team, he just loved to fight.

He was a natural showman, with confidence, charisma and skill.

He was made for wrestling.

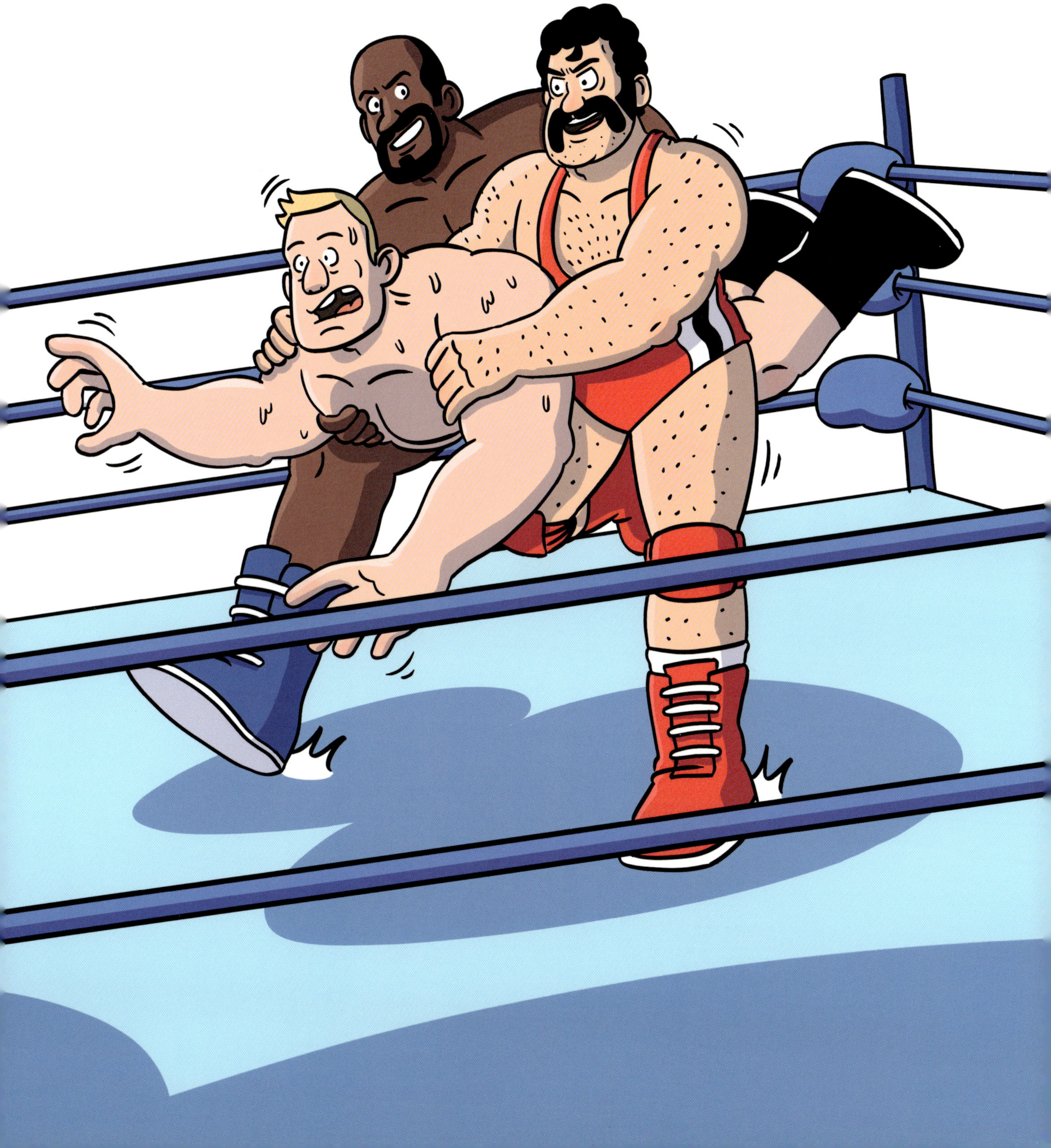

Orig spent a lot of time in Pakistan, where he wrestled in front of huge and enthusiastic crowds.

He often faced the famous Bholu Brothers who were very popular in their homeland.

Orig knew that stories needed heroes ... but also villains, and in Pakistan it was his job to be the bad guy.

Orig continued to play the villain for crowds in America, Africa and Asia. He was even given the nickname 'El Bandito' because his big moustache made him look like a Mexican bandit.

Back home, cheers and chants greeted Orig before every match. He was always a hero in Wales.

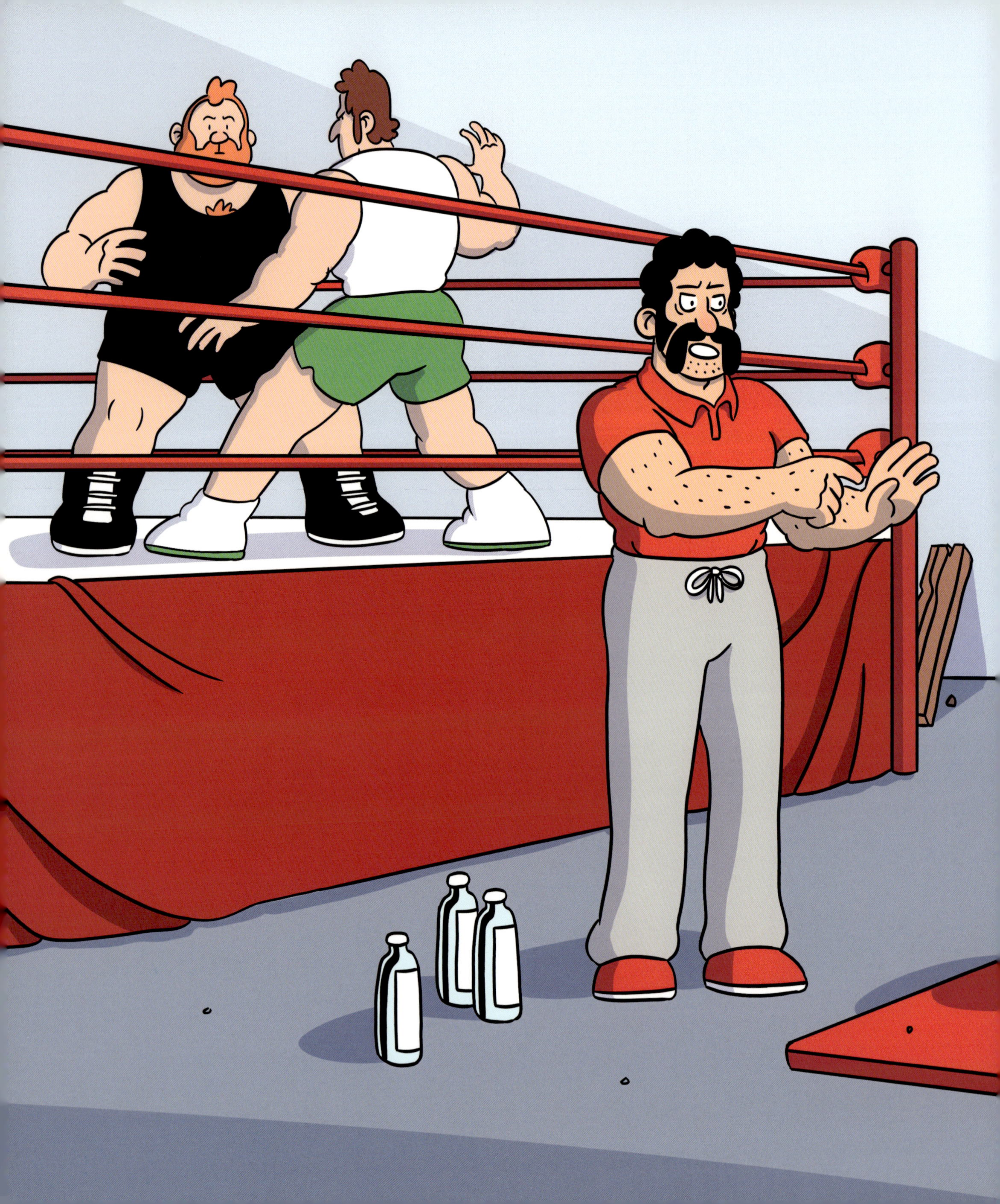

Orig began organising his own wrestling shows and also trained local Welsh wrestlers.

Some of the young trainees were shy and nervous, but Orig taught them to have belief in themselves and their country.

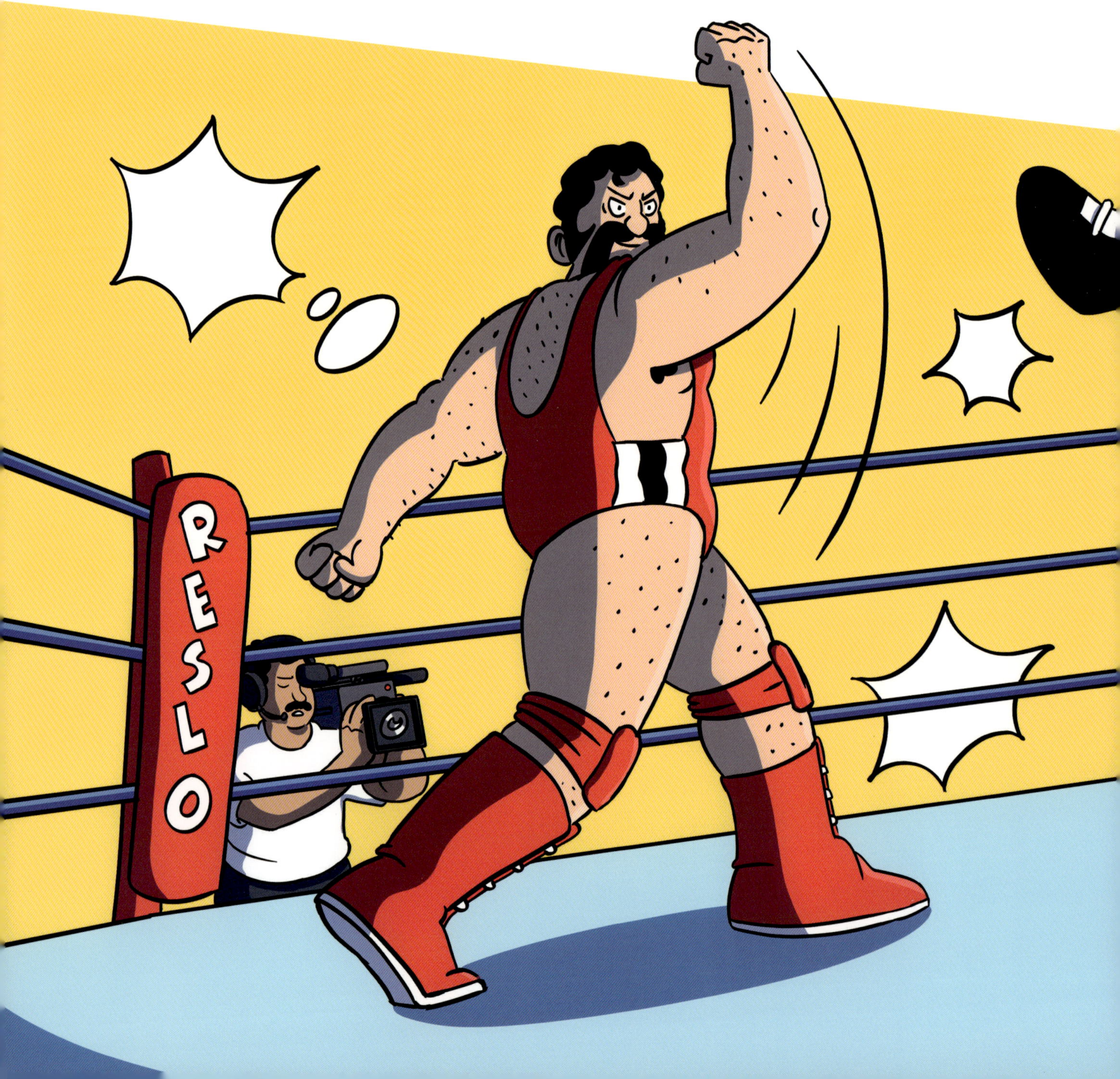
RESLO

Orig worked in front of the cameras and behind-the-scenes on the Welsh-language television programme, *Reslo*.

It was a unique and popular series featuring cage matches, women's wrestling and international stars.

During his long wrestling career Orig faced many opponents, from Fit Finlay and Lord Bertie Topham to Crusher Mason and Giant Haystacks.

Every one of them knew they'd been in a battle when they faced Orig Williams.

Despite all his exciting adventures, Orig was proudest of being husband to Wendy and father to Tara.

They were his favourite tag team.

We remember Orig Williams as the strongman who loved his family, his country and his language. He fought as hard for them as he did in the wrestling ring.

Read about more Welsh Wonders

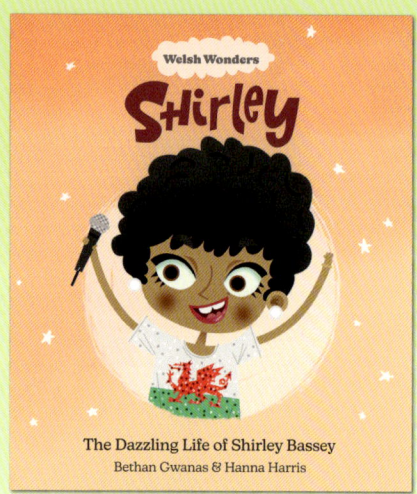

Shirley Bassey
The girl from Tiger Bay whose voice became famous around the world.

Cranogwen
Sarah Jane Rees was a sea captain, prize-winning poet, publisher, and inspiration!

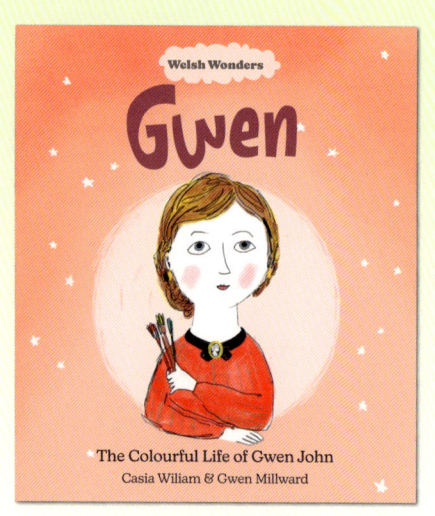

Gwen John
A shy but determined girl who loved to paint and followed her dream of being a famous artist.

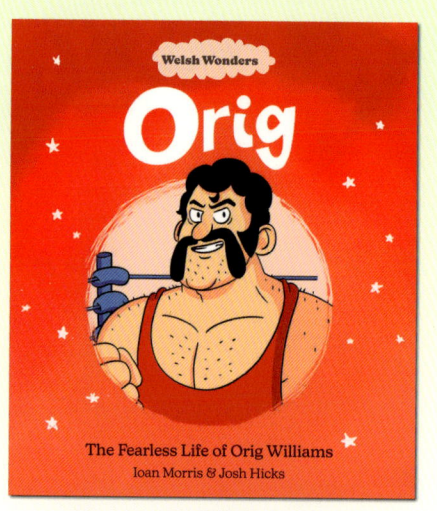

Orig Williams
The tough-guy wrestler with a heart of gold, known around the world as El Bandito!